Divine Decrees

Divine Decrees

ASCENDING THE COURTS OF HEAVEN

Bill Vincent

ArcanaVerse Books

Contents

1

Introduction

I firmly believe we are at the most pivotal moment in history. It feels as though certain elements are aligning, being set in order by divine grace. Often, we persistently pursue our goals, yet doors remain closed, and progress seems elusive. What's the missing piece? Could it be a divine verdict awaiting in the celestial courts? This thought crossed my mind as I sought divine guidance. As I delved into prayer, the notion of a heavenly court being in session was revealed to me.

No matter where you stand in your spiritual journey, I assure you, monumental breakthroughs are on the horizon for the faithful. Decisions are being made in the divine realm, decisions that will work in your favor, hallelujah. Do you believe in the power of prophetic proclamations? Indeed, such decrees carry immense power, an integral part of the heavenly court's proceedings. Let's delve into the concept of prophetic decrees.

Understanding the significance of issuing decrees that resonate with divine intent is crucial. While we have the freedom to declare anything, only the decrees aligned with God's will bear fruit. It's about discerning and declaring God's agenda for the current season, a revelation intertwined with the workings of the heavenly courts. Often, we speak of courts of praise without a true comprehension of the celestial dynamics. My previous works and teachings have explored the intricacies of the heavenly court system in great detail, navigating through its principles and ordinances.

However, it's not about repetitively preaching the old, but rather using it to unveil new revelations, hallelujah. Let's also touch upon the subject of angels. Their presence has been profoundly felt in revival meetings, signaling their active role in the divine scheme. If you doubt the existence of angels, then the entire concept of a heavenly court might elude you. Who do you think executes the divine decrees in heaven? Angels are the celestial agents at work. Prepare yourself for what's coming, hallelujah.

Furthermore, we will explore the significance of making decrees to engage the heavenly court, to counteract forces opposing God's plan, and to usher in restoration in our lives. Recall the creation narrative: Adam and Eve were instilled with dominion over the earthly realm, granted the authority to issue decrees. When Adam named the animals, he wasn't merely assigning labels; he was activating their divine essence through his words, functioning as a mouthpiece of God. This authority was not just a one-time delegation but a continuous empowerment to enact God's will on Earth.

This discourse is deeply rooted in scriptural references, enhancing the prophetic narrative. To provide a more comprehensive biblical context, we've included an additional chapter with scriptural references at the end of this section.

2

Chapter One: Reclaiming Authority

I firmly believe we are meant to reclaim the authority once bestowed upon us in the Garden of Eden. Do you share this belief? Thanks to Jesus' sacrifice, we have the right to do so. Adam and Eve may have faltered, allowing the devil to usurp their dominion, but does this define the entirety of the church? On Sundays, many gather to sing, listen to the word, and then return to their lives, only to repeat the cycle. Yet, they live not in the era of a resurrected Christ but in the shadow of a fallen Adam and Eve.

This morning, during a quiet moment, a divine message came to me: many love God, but fewer truly know Him. The church, in its entirety, has strayed from the essence of the gospel, the genuine power of God, settling instead for a semblance of the old faith. This nostalgia for the "old time religion" should not be about clinging to traditions but about returning to the dynamism of the early church, as depicted in the Book of Acts, where faith was alive and transformative.

The disobedience of Adam and Eve brought a curse upon humanity, stripping us of our dominion. Often, we underestimate the ripple effect of our decisions. While it's easy to critique Adam and Eve's choice, who amongst us can confidently say we would resist temptation in a similar paradise? We might judge from a distance, yet we haven't walked in their shoes. It's crucial, now more than ever, for the church to redeem itself and reestablish the heavenly court's support. We lost our authority to decree as kings, but God did not abandon us. He sent Jesus Christ to redeem us, allowing us to approach the throne of grace boldly and engage in the divine judicial system.

Through Jesus, we have been granted a dominion superior to that of the original garden, a spiritual authority over evil forces in the celestial realms. This world might not resemble heaven, but it's categorized as such biblically, with the devil and his minions occupying the second heaven. Our earthly sojourn is temporary, a transit point before the eternal. The true battle is spiritual, often requiring us to press through the resistance of the second heaven to experience the full glory of the third, where God reigns supreme.

The church must awaken from complacency, actively engaging in this spiritual warfare. We are called to be assertive, to invoke heaven's intervention in our reality. We possess the divine privilege to partake in the heavenly courtroom, where God's justice prevails over every accusation of the enemy. Aligning with this celestial justice system ensures that God's plans will always triumph over the adversary's schemes. It's a divine guarantee if approached with righteousness and faith.

3

Chapter Two: Angels Released

In this chapter, I want to delve into the concept of angels on a mission. Understand this: you have angels specifically assigned to you, waiting in the wings, ready to act upon the verdicts of the heavenly court. Picture this: a host of angels aligned by the throne, poised to carry out God's decrees. These celestial beings act upon the judgments that resonate in heaven. Consider the profound implication of this: what we bind on Earth is bound in heaven, what we loose on Earth is loosed in heaven.

When you declare, for instance, "Revival Ways of Glory Shall come forth now in the name of Jesus," it's not just words spoken. It's a decree that resonates, causing a heavenly echo. This echo ensures that what's proclaimed here manifests there. Imagine the heavens responding, with Peter catching your decree like a catcher in baseball, presenting it to God, and God affirming, "Let it be so." This isn't just about binding and loosing; it's about initiating a divine process that many have yet to fully grasp.

Once a decision is made in the celestial council, a divine messenger announces it, or an angel executes it. When you understand your identity in Him, when you grasp that you are a child of the King, you wield the authority to issue decrees that mobilize angels. They don't serve you per se; they serve His purpose. Your prophetic decrees transform into His words, and He is committed to fulfilling them. Psalm 103 verses 19-21 encapsulates this beautifully, describing how angels excel in strength, executing His word, and performing His will.

Angels are not idle; they are designed for God's judicial system. Yet, the church has underutilized this celestial workforce. These angels are more than ready to act, almost as if they've been waiting on the sidelines. We are called to declare things into existence, to invoke the unseen into the seen realm. This is not mere wishful thinking; it's about understanding and engaging with the heavenly judicial system.

When a verdict is pronounced in the heavenly court, it's as binding and definitive as any earthly court's decree. While the manifestation of that verdict might undergo a process, the outcome is assured. If heaven has decreed restitution for what was lost or stolen, angels are dispatched to ensure that restoration.

I feel compelled by the Spirit to declare: those who embrace this truth will see restitution. Financial dues, long-awaited healings, and salvation for loved ones are within reach. It's time to actively engage with the heavenly court, not just for temporary salvation but for eternal transformation. It's getting intense, and it's essential that we delve deeper into the workings of the heavenly court system.

4

〜

Chapter Three: Make Decrees

Our reluctance to issue decrees, as instructed by God, impedes angels from fulfilling their roles in our lives. It's our responsibility to voice these decrees, aligning our proclamations with God's word and the destiny He has spoken over us. It's not merely about uttering words; it's about prophesying life into our circumstances, assuming our roles as ambassadors and enacting kingly judgments.

Let me share a personal anecdote. On a trip to Florida, where I often visited, I was given a timeshare at a resort. That weekend, my sermon was about being ambassadors for Christ. Upon arrival, I was directed to a parking space marked 'Ambassador'. This wasn't a co-incidence; it was a divine affirmation, reminding me of our reserved place in heaven, our legal entitlement as God's children.

God urges us to abandon unrighteous judgments, to view our situations not through the lens of human limitation but through faith and divine insight. Even when our financial reality seems bleak, faith and divine intervention can turn the tide. This is about breaking the enemy's stronghold over our minds, releasing decrees that align with God's will, and unlocking the doors to breakthroughs. God has provided us the key – our voice, our decrees – and it's up to us to utilize it.

Psalm 82 sheds light on this truth, portraying God as the judge among the mighty, questioning the duration of unjust judgments and favoritism towards the wicked. We, the 'little gods', are part of this narrative, not diminishing God's glory but rather amplifying it through our association with Him. Just like the son of a king enjoys certain diplomatic immunities, we, as children of the Most High, operate under a divine jurisdiction. Our earthly systems even reflect this understanding, granting certain immunities to those from foreign courts.

God is examining our judgments, our proclamations, to liberate the oppressed and show mercy to those in need. He challenges us to defend the marginalized, to bring justice to the afflicted, ushering in an era of power evangelism. We are called to minister to the down-trodden, to decree in the heavenly court on their behalf, especially when they lack the means to do so themselves.

Regrettably, the church often falls short in this mission, casting aside those who don't fit the conventional mold. This isn't justice; this isn't love. Regardless of someone's appearance or past, they should find a sanctuary in the church. In the coming years, expect more individuals drawn by the Holy Spirit, marked by their unique journeys and appearances. It's our duty to welcome them, lest we grieve the Holy Spirit who drew them to us.

Remember, when we first step into a church, often carrying a burden of sin, it's a moment of vulnerability and courage. God's mercy and Jesus' sacrifice afford us the right to be there. As God declares in the scriptures, we are judges, children of the Most High, tasked with enacting His justice and love on Earth.

5

Chapter Four: God's Judgment

In this chapter, I delve into the profound responsibility bestowed upon us by God – the duty to enact justice, especially for the marginalized. We live in a time where too many children are growing up without fathers, a situation that deeply troubles me. For instance, consider a man who abandons his family just after the birth of his child, driven by jealousy over the attention the infant receives. Such actions leave an indelible mark on the family, reinforcing the harsh reality that child support, however necessary, can never replace the presence and guidance of a father.

Asaph, in his Psalm, cries out, "Arise, O God, judge the earth; for You shall inherit all nations." This is a plea for divine intervention, an acknowledgment of our failure to administer justice. If we desire righteousness to prevail, we must be proactive, declaring it through our decrees. The current state of our nation, marred by economic turmoil and moral decline, can be seen as a reflection of our collective choices and, perhaps, a form of divine judgment.

We have built idols within the church, straying from our

foundational truths. Despite this, we are reminded that God has appointed us as 'mighty ones,' entrusted us with the authority to judge, an authority that originates from Him. We are called to participate in the heavenly court system, to invoke God's restorative power for the oppressed and bound, and this requires us to boldly declare prophetic decrees.

In the United States, the principle of 'innocent until proven guilty' underscores the power of judicial decrees. Similarly, in the spiritual realm, we are the 'little G's,' the judges called to address the injustices around us, whether it be towards a homeless individual or someone wronged in any way. Our decrees can bring forth justice, echoing in the heavenly court.

It's crucial to understand that our decrees, aligned with God's word, carry immense power unless countered by a higher divine decree. We are entrusted with the duty to care for the marginalized – the widows, the orphans, the fatherless, and the poor. Our role is not just to uphold righteousness within the church but to extend it to all humanity, embracing even those who may appear different or unwelcome.

As we tread this path, it's important to remember that the efficacy of our decrees hinges on the purity of our hearts and our alignment with God's will. Repentance and a heart cleansed of any malice or bitterness are prerequisites for our decrees to bear fruit. We must approach the heavenly court with a spirit of humility and readiness to receive God's wisdom and guidance.

In closing, let us prepare our hearts, repent, and ensure they are aligned with God's righteousness. As we decree, let us do so with the confidence that the entirety of heaven supports the words we utter, for the heavenly court is indeed in session. Let this be a time of worship, of cleansing, and of bold declarations. Embrace the changes God is about to bring into your life and the lives of others through your faithful decrees.

6

～

Chapter Five: Apostolic Breakthrough Decrees

Apostolic decrees transcend ordinary declarations, embodying a higher realm of divine authority. These decrees, divinely sanctioned and dispatched from heaven, wield immense power to establish God's justice and dismantle the adversary's destructive schemes. They're akin to a preemptive strike in the spiritual realm.

God has impressed upon me the significance of apostolic declarations, drawing my attention to Isaiah 61:2. This scripture heralds a divine mandate for the forthcoming years: to proclaim the year of the Lord's favor, a season of divine Jubilee. This mandate empowers us to declare a time of comprehensive deliverance, debt cancellation, and liberation from any form of bondage. Invoking "Jubilee" sets into motion a divine force, aligning our lives with God's order.

The anointing we receive transcends temporal constraints. When God's word is proclaimed, heavenly angels spring into action, bestowing upon us a supernatural strength previously unknown. Moreover, invoking "Favor" initiates a divine shift, attracting God's grace like a tangible mantle descending from the heavens.

However, obtaining favor involves adherence to certain principles. It's not merely about seeking favor; it's about engaging with God in a profound and passionate manner. While God's love is unconditional, the intensity of our pursuit can elevate the favor we receive. This favor is not stagnant; it grows through obedience and fervent seeking, just as Jesus and King David experienced an increase in favor through their devotion and pursuit of God.

Now, let's delve deeper into the role of apostolic decrees in God's judicial system. These decrees empower us to call the heavenly court into session, to stand as witnesses against injustice. We are anointed to declare God's vindication, defending against criticism or censure. This anointing allows us to engage with the heavenly court, where the Holy Spirit acts as our advocate, addressing matters related to our destiny and injustices we face.

We are called not only to seek justice for ourselves but also to invoke divine judgment against our adversaries. This judicial engagement is rooted in a deep understanding of God's heavenly court, described in scriptures through various terms like Divine Council, Counsel of El, Council of Yahweh, and Council of the Holy Ones. This divine council comprises a multitude of heavenly beings, including God, hosts of heaven, cloud of witnesses, living prophets and believers, and even adversaries.

The divine counsel of God, wherein heavenly beings engage with God's wisdom, can manifest in various earthly and celestial settings, such as mountains, temples, or tabernacles. The Apostle John's vision in Revelation chapters 4 and 5 vividly illustrates this. He witnesses the throne of God, surrounded by a sea of glass, four living creatures, and twenty-four elders in a scene of profound worship. This heavenly setting, while primarily a place of worship, also transforms into a courtroom where divine judgments are dispensed.

Scriptures like Daniel 7 and Revelation 4 offer detailed depictions of the throne room, revealing both the Ancient of Days and the Son of Man in their governmental authority. Interestingly, while both Daniel and John describe the presence of the Lamb of God and four living creatures, their visions differ in certain aspects, such as the mobility of the throne and the appearance of the living creatures. These prophetic insights underscore the dynamic and multifaceted nature of God's throne, a celestial chariot propelled by the living creatures, reminiscent of the Levitical priests carrying the Ark of the Covenant, symbolizing God's omnipresence.

David's directive in 1 Chronicles 15:2 sets the stage for understanding the sacredness of God's presence, likening the transport of the Ark to the dynamic nature of the Throne Room, reminiscent of the Tabernacle of Moses and Solomon's Temple. This imagery evokes a profound reverence for the Throne of God, a symbol of His presence, which, like the Ark, moves as God's presence moves.

The Divine Council Room, or the Heavenly Court, is an extension of this sacred space. It's a venue for divine judgments, yet it's more than a court; it's also a place of worship. Interestingly, while the devil can access the Throne of Judgment to levy accusations against believers, he's barred from the Throne Room of Worship. We see this dynamic interplay in 1 Kings 22:19-23, where the prophet Micaiah unveils a court session in heaven, and an evil spirit is permitted to execute part of God's sovereign plan.

Leaders like Joshua and Jeremiah, as seen in the scriptures, had access to this Divine Council Room. Zechariah 3:7 portrays Joshua standing before the Lord in the heavenly courts, granted the privilege to walk among the council after being cleansed and robed in righteousness. Jeremiah is acknowledged in Jeremiah 23:18-20 as one who stood in the Lord's counsel and proclaimed His judgments.

The heavenly decrees we pronounce on earth are executed by angels, as King David poetically describes in Psalms 103:19-21. Our responsibility to make these decrees is profound; failing to do so limits the intervention of these celestial beings in our lives. God calls us to render righteous judgments, abstaining from superficial, human perspectives.

Psalms 82:1 reveals God standing in the congregation of the mighty, adjudicating among the 'little gods,'—us. We are designated as judges, rulers, or sons of God, entrusted with the power to make prophetic proclamations. Our judgments have the potential to liberate captives and extend mercy to the underserved. Asaph's plea in Psalms 82:8 underscores the urgency of our divine mandate to invoke God's judgment on earth, as our efforts alone fall short in administering true justice.

In the battlefield of life, we often feel beleaguered, contending against formidable forces. The prophecies of Daniel, especially Daniel 7:21-22, depict this spiritual warfare, where the saints face oppression until the Ancient of Days intervenes, passing judgment in favor of the saints and bestowing upon them the kingdom. Our role in this cosmic battle is pivotal; through our decrees, aligned with God's will, we beckon the intervention of the Divine Council, ushering in God's righteous judgments and fostering the restoration and liberation of the oppressed. This profound collaboration between the earthly and the divine encapsulates our calling as stewards of the Heavenly Court, a calling that demands our utmost faith, diligence, and alignment with God's sovereign will.

When the Ancient of Days presides over judgment, we stand at the cusp of justice. Today, this very moment, we have the opportunity to ascend to the courts of heaven, to present our case before the Judge of all. With apostolic declarations on our lips, we can act as God's appointed stewards on Earth. As we declare, "Exaltation will come!" we empower God to uplift the downtrodden and liberate those ensnared. When we proclaim, "Restore!" we invoke God's restorative anointing, compelling not just a return, but a multiplication of what was lost or broken.

Before we petition the courts of heaven, reflect on every facet of your life where you yearn for breakthrough. Perhaps it's your inheritance being withheld, your health under siege, or any injustice you've strived to counter single-handedly. In these moments, remember, it's not our place to seek vengeance; we need God to champion our cause.

As we stand in the heavenly courtroom, each decree we pronounce, aligned with God's will, activates the angelic hosts. They either announce God's verdict or enact His judgment. Remember, in the Old Testament, courts adjudicated over life, death, destiny, kingship, and inheritance. Today, we too have the authority to petition the Ancient of Days for divine judgment in these critical aspects of our lives.

I've witnessed the power of such decrees firsthand. Miraculous testimonies of financial restitution and other breakthroughs have followed apostolic declarations made in faith.

So now, let us confidently approach God's throne. Present your case, recall prophetic promises, and articulate each injustice. God entrusts us with the mission to proclaim freedom to the captives and open prison doors. Our words carry the power to bring justice and mercy to the downtrodden and forgotten. As we intercede today, let's petition God for judgment and favor in our lives:

"God, we stand before the court of heaven, petitioning You, the righteous Judge. We represent the voices of the oppressed and the afflicted, seeking Your divine judgment and vindication. You are the God who overcomes reproach, the God who advocates for Your people. Today, we respectfully present our petitions, requesting the attention of the heavenly council. We stand united, asking for Your divine intervention where it's most needed.

Open the courts of heaven. Let the session commence. We decree: 'Exaltation will come! Restore! Restore! Restore!' We proclaim Your word over every loss, commanding the adversary to relinquish what he has stolen. We declare Your day of vengeance, the year of Your favor, our year of Jubilee. We pronounce blessings of divine favor: 'Favor! Favor! Favor!' We feel Your glory, Lord!

We commission the angelic hosts to enforce Your judgment, to reclaim our divine destiny, and to vanquish every

demonic force opposing our inheritance. In the authority of Jesus' name, we dismantle every stronghold and scheme set against us. We assert our kingship over all resistance, knowing You, O God, will render judgment in favor of Your saints.

We thank You, Lord, for the victory that is ours. We await the triumphant execution of Your justice, as Your angels move to restore, to liberate, and to establish the fullness of Your blessings in our lives. We stand in faith, declaring: 'Restore! Restore! Restore!' and we embrace the certainty of Your favor. This is our acceptable year, the year of Your favor, our season of Jubilee.

We decree: 'Favor! Favor! Favor!' and anticipate the manifestation of Your vengeance against every injustice. We bask in Your glory, confident in the angelic enforcement of Your righteous decrees.

May Your warring angels thwart every enemy, securing our rightful inheritance and affirming our destiny as Your children. We await Your judgment, O Ancient of Days, in favor of the saints. We rejoice in advance for the victory that is assuredly ours in Christ Jesus. Amen."

7

About the Author

Diving deep into the realms of spiritual awakening, Bill Vincent embodies a connection with the Supernatural that spans over three decades. With a robust prophetic anointing, he has dedicated his life to ministry, serving as a guiding light and a pillar of strength in Revival Waves of Glory Ministries.

Bill Vincent is not just a Minister but a prolific Author, contributing to the spiritual enlightenment of many through his diverse range of writings and teachings. His work encompasses themes of deliverance, fostering the presence of God, and shaping Apostolic, cutting-edge Church structure. His insights are drawn from a wellspring of experience, steeped in Revival, and fine-tuned by a profound Spiritual Sensitivity.

In his relentless pursuit of God's Presence and his commitment to sustaining Revival, Bill focuses primarily on inviting divine encounters and maintaining a spiritual atmosphere ripe for transformation. His extensive library of over 125 books serves as a beacon of hope, guiding countless individuals in overcoming the shackles of Satan and embracing the light of God.

Revival Waves of Glory Ministries is not your typical church – it's a prophetic ministry, a sanctuary where the Holy Spirit is given the freedom to move as He wills. Our sermons, a blend of divine wisdom and revelation, can be experienced on Rumble, immersing you in the transformative power of the Word: https://rumble.com/c/revivalwavesofgloryministriesbillvincent

For a deeper exploration into our teachings, visions, and the manifold grace of God, visit https://www.revivalwavesofglorymin-istries.com/.

Embark on a journey of spiritual discovery with Bill Vincent, and let the waves of revival wash over you, unveiling the divine power and boundless love of God!

Podcast: https://podcasters.spotify.com/pod/show/bill-vincent2

Rumble: https://rumble.com/c/revivalwavesofgloryministriesbil-lvincent

Be sure to check out our new videos **Downloads From Heaven!**